The Girl on the Train

Paula Hawkins

A

SUMMARY, ANALYSIS & REVIEW

Note to Readers:

This is a Summary & Analysis of *The Girl on the Train*, by Paula Hawkins. You are encouraged to buy the full version.

TABLE OF CONTENTS

INTRODUCTION

Rachel Watson has spent years in an alcoholic depression since her husband left her for another woman. Now she wiles away her days riding the commuter train to and from London, despite having been fired from her job months ago. The train makes a daily stop by her old neighborhood and it is here she spies a couple appearing to be living a perfect life from a beautiful home. She begins to fantasize about the couple, 'Jess' and 'Jason,' inventing little lives and backstories for them to keep her mind off her own troubles.

But that fantasy shatters when she witnesses 'Jess' kissing another man. And the following day, when 'Jess' disappears, Rachel begins to wonder if she might be the only one with information that could help find her.

Delving headfirst into the investigation, Rachel becomes obsessed with the case and deeply intertwined with all the parties involved. All the while, she tries desperately to remember the night of the disappearance, sifting through the drunken haze of her memory in search of answers.

Rachel learns that the perfect lives of 'Jess' and 'Jason' maybe weren't so perfect after all. As the case grows more complicated each day, Rachel's suspicions shift rapidly from one person to the next. And when the truth finally is brought to light, it may be more than she ever bargained for.

BOOK REVIEW

Paula Hawkins' debut novel, *The Girl on the Train*, is a suspenseful thrillerwith a complex plot, shocking twists and an ending that will both stun and leave the reader wanting more. Rachel Watson is a depressed drunkard living vicariously through others to avoid facing her own miserable life. She doesn't even know the couple she watches each morning through the commuter train window, yet she fantasizes about the fictionalized 'Jess' and 'Jason' as though they were friends. When 'Jess' disappears without a trace, Rachel becomes obsessed with the investigation. Believing she alone may hold key information to the missing woman's whereabouts, she begins some detective work of her own.

Suspense, intrigue, drama, and murder, all entangled together into one giant knot that is begging to be unraveled. Hawkins' expertly writes a gripping tale of suspense, intrigue, drama and murder with intricate details that keep the reader guessing throughout. The plot comes together at just the right time to leave no question unanswered.

Character development is paces such that only a little detail is divulged at a time, maintaining suspense. In the end, the characters are fleshed out perfectly, fulfilling their roles in the story with ease.

Each chapter is told in a first-person perspective, alternating among Rachel's, Megan's and Anna's. Megan's chapters take place several months prior to the stories Rachel and Anna narrate, but Hawkins handles the time-shifting smoothly. Giving each woman her own voice allows for some flexibility in the storytelling and provides the opportunity to understand first-hand their individual motivations.

The Girl on the Train is a strong debut for Hawkins and is sure to whet the appetites of readers in the thriller genre, leaving them anxiously awaiting Hawkins' sophomore project.

SETTING FOR THE STORY

The Girl on the Train takes place just outside of London, with the dreary English weather emphasizing Rachel's depressed state. The gloominess of the weather so well known to the British Isles also adds a bit of a dark and mysterious air to a suspenseful story centered on lies, betrayal and murder.

The commuter train that carries Rachel into and out of London each day is a setting of its own, providing her a front row seat for the suburban life of 'Jess' and 'Jason' which she has become so fascinated with. In many ways, the train has become a second home to Rachel. It's a safe place for her to hide away from the world, sitting amongst strangers who cannot hold her accountable for her poor life choices. It also allows her to stay somewhat connected with her ex-husband, as she routinely passes by his home and therefore can always feel close to him.

The town of Witney is the epitome of suburbia. It's a place where people raise their families in matching cookie-cutter houses, taking comfort in their safe surroundings. For Rachel, Witney represents stability. It reminds her of the life that she has lost, the one where she is still a wife, still employed, and still sober. For Megan, the monotony of suburban life in Witney is stifling. She craves anything but the predictability of her days as a housewife. But the false sense of security Witney provides is crudely ripped away with the disappearance - the murder - of one of its own residents.

STORY PLOT ANALYSIS

The Girl on the Train presents a complex, braided plot that follows three narrative foci – Rachel, Megan and Anna – back and forth across the summers of 2012 and 2013. While the motion through time might otherwise be confusing, Hawkins announces that motion clearly in the headings that divide each chapter by days and parts of the day. The narrowed focus on specific moments in time allows for intensive character development, while the motion through broader spans of time creates the impression that the excerpted moments are representative of the whole, allowing the reader to follow easily without becoming mired in minutiae that do not support the story.

MAIN & SECONDARY CHARACTER LIST

Main Characters

- Rachel Watson - heroine
- Tom Watson – Rachel's ex-husband
- Anna Boyd Watson – Tom's new wife
- Megan Hipwell – Rachel's "Jess"
- Scott Hipwell – Megan's husband and Rachel's "Jason"
- Dr. Kamal Abdic – Megan's therapist
- Detective Inspector Gaskill – investigator in the disappearance of Megan Hipwell
- Detective Sergeant Riley – investigator in the disappearance of Megan Hipwell
- Cathy – Rachel's college friend and flatmate in Ashbury

Secondary Characters

- Evie Watson – Tom and Anna’s baby daughter
- Damien – Cathy’s boyfriend
- Andy – a man Rachel meets on the train
- Tara – Megan’s friend
- Craig “Mac” McKenzie – Megan’s ex-boyfriend
- Elizabeth “Libby” – Megan’s deceased baby daughter
- Martin Miles – Rachel’s former boss

BOOK OVERVIEW & STORY ANALYSIS

Below appears a summary of the text, with some analytical comments interspersed.

Chapter 1 - Rachel

As Rachel rides the commuter train into London, she notices a pile of discarded clothing along the side of the tracks, wondering about them and how they came to be there long after the train has passed. She pays particular attention to one house on the route, watching the couple who resides there as they carry on with their day. Although she does not know them, she imagines their names are Jason and Jess, and she invents lives and characteristics for them. She does not like to remember the home only four houses down from theirs, the one that she shared with her former husband, Tom. Now she resides in a flat with her old college friend Cathy, where she spends most of her time drunk. One evening, Rachel places multiple drunken calls to Tom, professing her unending love for him on his voicemail. Tom returns the call, asks her to stop ringing him and encourages her to go to an AA meeting.

Chapter 2 - Megan

Megan sits and listens to the commuter train go by each morning, imagining exotic travels for those on board, even though she knows it's just carrying them to work. She feels restless as a housewife and yearns for her former job, managing an art gallery which has since closed. In an effort to get out of the house, she takes a position as a nanny for her neighbors, Tom and Anna Watson. But she quits the job soon after, feeling useless as the mother is there all day alongside her. She thinks of her brother, Ben, and all the adventures they had planned before his untimely death. She wonders if the pain of his passing is the cause of her own unhappiness and begins to see a therapist. She also considers calling on the Watsons, but decides against it.

Chapter 3 - Rachel

Rachel witnesses 'Jess' kissing a strange man and feels a sense of betrayal that 'Jess' would cheat on 'Jason.' Rachel remembers the day she found out Tom was having an affair via email messages between him and his mistress, Anna. Rachel drinks away a lonely Saturday and, on impulse, decides to ride the train past the house where 'Jess' and 'Jason' live, hoping to catch a glimpse of what is going on at home. The next thing she knows, she is waking up in her bed, bruised and bloodied, but with no memory of the night before. Tom has left her an angry voicemail, accusing her of frightening his wife, but Rachel can't remember what it is that she did. Cathy arrives home to find Rachel's vomit on the floor and asks her to move out.

]

Chapter 4 - Megan

Megan continues to struggle in her life at home and begins to be sexually involved with her therapist, Kamal. She uses Tara to hide her indiscretions from Scott.

Chapter 5 – Rachel

Rachel receives formal eviction notice from Cathy and proceeds to London. She sees 'Jason' as she passes his home on the train. That evening finds Rachel in the emergency room after getting hit by a taxi. She was distracted by an article she saw online with a photo of 'Jess,' or rather, Megan Hipwell, who has been reported as missing.

Chapter 6 - Megan

Megan is making headway in her therapy with Kamal, but finds she still holds back because she feels guilty confiding things to him that she can't even share with her husband. She tells Kamal of her happiness in the relationship with her ex, Mac, and how he broke her heart. Scott had seen that she had been searching for Mac on the internet and confronted her, leading to a heated argument. When Megan tells Kamal about this incident, he suggests that perhaps Scott is emotionally abusive and that she fears him. After the session, she follows Kamal home and knocks on his door, kissing him when he opens it and spending the night with him.

Chapter 7 - Rachel

Rachel returns to her old neighborhood of Witney in hopes that being there will jog her memory of what happened the night she frightened Anna. She has a flashback while in the underpass, remembering sitting with bloody hands. She also remembers a male train passenger with reddish hair, but can't recall if he was more than a friendly face. She is keeping tabs on Megan's disappearance as the news spreads nationally. When Rachel returns home, Gaskill is there to question her about her activities from the night that Megan went missing. She is less than honest with many of her answers, prompting her to go to the police station the following day to set the record straight. The detectives question her about an incident involving her breaking into Tom and Anna's home and taking their newborn daughter. Rachel reflects on her inability to have children and how this sorrow led through drinking to losing Tom. But she denies that was how the incident went down and begins to feel the detectives targeting her as a suspect, so she informs them of Megan's extramarital lover. She also tries to reach out to Scott, and she continues to try to piece her memories together.

Chapter 8 - Megan

Megan urges Kamal to run away with her, but he refuses before opening up to her. She knows that she loves Scott, but is too stifled by their conventional life and needs the freedom.

Chapter 9 - Rachel

Rachel's role in the case is enough to keep her sober for three days, her fascination with the investigation and her purpose in it fueling her newfound sobriety. It is short-lived, as she has celebratory drinks after a successful meeting with Gaskill, in which she identifies Megan's lover in a photograph. Drunk, she sends a scathing email to Tom, which she regrets come morning. As she sits to write an apology, she receives an email from Scott, and, at his request, Rachel goes to his house to tell him about Megan's affair.

Chapter 10 - Anna

Anna celebrates a quiet birthday at home, reflecting on how lucky she is to have married Tom and had Evie. As the day winds down, she looks outside and sees a woman walking down the street, instantly knowing who it is. When Tom asks her what is wrong, she waves it off as nothing.

Chapter 11 -Rachel

Rachel tries to sneak by Tom and Anna's house undetected on her way to Scott's. She tells Scott that she saw Megan kissing another man. Scott shows Rachel a couple of photos that match the description she gave of the lover and she is able to identify the other man as Kamal. The following day, Scott rings her to thank her for coming forward. Taking comfort in their conversation, he admits to the argument he and Megan had the night she disappeared and his guilt for having treating her poorly. The following morning while on the train, Rachel sees an article that says a man has been arrested in regards to Megan's disappearance. She abruptly departs at the Witney station and runs to Scott's house. Just as she is debating whether to knock, he opens the door and pulls her inside.

Chapter 12 - Megan

Megan is upset at being ignored by her lover, feeling as though he has rejected her. She arrives at her therapy session enraged and attempts unsuccessfully to force herself on Kamal. He has to forcefully remove her hands from him, leaving bruises on her arms. She kisses him and bites his lip until it bleeds. She leaves the session and begins to plot her revenge at having been cast aside.

Chapter 13 - Rachel

Scott tells Rachel she shouldn't be there as his home is being staked out by the media. He informs her that the police have arrested Kamal and then his mother escorts her out. Just as she steps outside, she is spotted by Tom and Anna as they are walking down the street.

Chapter 14 - Anna

Anna is shaken after seeing Rachel departing Scott's house. She tries to convince Tom they should call the police, but he dissuades her and promises he will call her to find out what she was doing in the neighborhood.

Chapter 15 – Rachel

Due to insufficient evidence, Kamal is eventually released without charges being filed. An angry Scott calls Rachel after learning from Detective Riley that Rachel is an alcoholic and possibly mentally unstable. Rachel sinks into a depression, suffering from incessant nightmares that she can't quite decipher. She calls Tom hoping to get some clarification regarding the events of the night Megan disappeared. He asks her why she was at Scott's, and she tells him of Megan's affair. Grasping at straws to piece together the events from that night, Rachel goes to the train station at Witney hoping to run into the man from the train with the reddish hair. Instead, she sees Scott and apologizes for not being forthcoming about her situation. Several days later, the news reports that a body believed to be Megan Hipwell's has been discovered in the wood not far from her home.

Chapter 16 - Megan

Megan continues to feel suffocated by life as a housewife. Her thoughts are consumed with running away and starting over somewhere else. She decides to seek out Kamal and apologize. She wants to tell him the secret which weighs so heavily on her shoulders. He accepts her apology and agrees to listen. She confides that while she was with Mac, she became pregnant. They didn't want Libby, but she was born and they accepted the change. One cold night after an argument, Mac stormed out and Megan began drinking against the chill. She took a bath to warm herself and Libby, but fell asleep, only to wake up to her baby having drowned.

Chapter 17 - Rachel

After strange dreams, Rachel rides the train into London to have lunch with her mother, having drunk against doing so. On the train ride home, the man with the reddish hair sits beside her. She recognizes the scent of his aftershave and for a moment she catches a glimpse of a memory from the night Megan went missing. She feels a sense of fear that she can't quite identify and hastily leaves the man, walking to the front train car to get away from him. Still not able to piece together the memory through the alcoholic fog in her head, she has a brief recollection of Anna being there that night.

Chapter 18 - Anna

Anna muses on the burdens and joys of parenthood, trying to distract herself form thoughts of Megan. She is also paranoid about Rachel coming around, not fully convinced she wasn't somehow involved in Megan's disappearance since she was stumbling around the neighborhood in a drunken stupor that very same night. When she brings this to Riley's attention, the officer assures her that Rachel is nothing more than a lonely woman who is desperate to be a part of something.

Chapter 19 - Rachel

Rachel wakes from more dreams and rehearses events before questioning Scott about Megan's relationship with Anna. She tells him that she was in Witney the night Megan disappeared and recalls possibly seeing Anna by the underpass. Scott grows angry that Rachel is trying to manipulate her issues with Tom to coincide with Megan's death. He tells her the police suspect him as the murderer, Kamal's statements painting him as emotionally abusive. He appeals to Rachel to try and remember anything she can about that night to help him. Rachel hastily schedules a therapy session with Kamal, hoping to catch a glimpse of the monster that he is. Instead, she finds him attentive and warm and ends up spilling the story of her unraveling life out to him. Days later, Rachel spots the latest headline about Megan, wondering whether she was a child killer.

Chapter 20 - Anna

Anna's friends tell her about Megan possibly being a child killer and she is badly shaken. Haunted by memories of both Rachel and Megan in her house, she desperately tries to convince Tom to move; they cannot afford to.

Chapter 21 - Rachel

As she showers against the heat, Rachel takes a call from Scott; he is panicked and asks if he can hide from paparazzi at her house. He has learned that Megan was pregnant when she was killed and is grieved. Rachel attends another session with Kamal and confides that her barrenness that drove her to drink. She finds him comforting, which conflicts with her perception of him as Megan's killer. The body of Megan's baby, Libby, has been found just where the source said it would be. Scott is distraught and asks Rachel if she will come see him.

Chapter 22 - Megan

Megan returns to Kamal to finish telling him about Libby, noting where she and Mac buried the baby the following day and how he left her. Kamal tries to convince her to contact Mac to get some closureand tells her this is the last time they will see each other before sending her home. As she leaves, she stumbles outside and cuts her hand on the pavement, leaving a small bit of blood behind.

Chapter 23 - Rachel

Rachel wakes abed with Scott after they spent the night drinking and having sex. She feels guilty because she realizes it's her fictitious 'Jason' that she wanted to spend the night with and she allowed herself to get caught up in that fantasy. As Rachel leaves Scott's house, she spots Anna, who hurries away from her in fear.

Chapter 24 - Anna

Anna mentions seeing Rachel to Tom and suggests they get a restraining order, but he points out that Rachel isn't actually harassing them. Anna wearies of Tom putting her off and promising to take care of things, so she decides the next time she sees Rachel in the neighborhood, she will report it to Riley.

Chapter 25 - Rachel

Tom and Rachel go for a drive and talk. He is concerned about her relationship with Scott and makes her promise to stay away from him. She feels elated that he cares about her well-being and that he seems a little jealous. Rachel has another session with Kamal and inquires about recovering lost memories through hypnosis. She tells him about an incident in her marriage when Tom said she tried to attack him with a golf club. Though she didn't remember it, something later triggered a slight recollection of her emotions in that moment and it wasn't anger she had felt, but fear. The dots don't connect with the story Tom told her had occurred and she is confused. Rachel returns to Witney to try to recall more of the night Megan disappeared. Standing in the underpass, she recalls seeing Anna walking away from her towards Tom's car.

Chapter 26 - Anna

Anna rehearses her taking Tom from Rachel and later sees her watching from across the street, which unsettles her. She begins to doubt Tom is trying as hard as he claims to get his ex-wife out of their lives and decides to advise Riley of the situation. When she tells Tom of the incident, she catches him in a lie about having met up with Rachel when he originally said he only spoke to her on the phone. Although he quickly comes clean, it leads to doubts as she recalls all the lies Tom told to Rachel when he and Anna were having their affair. As the day goes on, the doubts magnify and Anna finds herself trying to guess the password to Tom's laptop.

Chapter 27 - Rachel

Scott distracts Rachel from a job interview, telling her the DNA results prove the baby Megan was carrying was not his or Kamal's. Riley has told Scott that Rachel lied to him about her connection with Megan. He is furious with her and becomes increasingly aggressive, grabbing her and forcing her into an upstairs bedroom. While she is trapped, he goes through her belongings and finds all her notes on the investigation. He eventually lets her out and orders her to leave his house. She runs to Tom's and knocks at his door, but when no one answers, she just leaves a note for him. Once home, she calls the police and tells Riley of the incident, now fully suspecting Scott may have been capable of Megan's murder. She runs into the man with the reddish hair from the train, Andy, and asks him what happened on the night she first met him, the night Megan disappeared. He says she had argued with Tom and he saw Tom and a woman drive off together. Rachel calls Tom to clarify and he is angry with her for calling. He sticks to his original story and tells her not to call anymore. As she drifts towards sleep later that night, she has a flash of a memory of being attacked.

Chapter 28 - Anna

Anna reflects on entanglements and notes having been home the night Rachel left the note for Tom and ignoring her at the door. She kept the note along with her log of Rachel's harassment. Tom confronts her about hiding the letter from him then leaves for the gym after their quarrel. Feeling insecure, Anna goes back to snooping on his laptop, managing to guess the password only to find nothing incriminating. She then notices Tom has forgotten his gym bag – and a mobile phone she has never seen. She starts to believe he and Rachel are having an affair behind her back, but the pieces don't completely add up. She listens to the voicemail greeting on the phone and hears another woman's voice.

Chapter 29 - Rachel

Rachel pieces together some memories, realizing the twisted versions of the events Tom told her had been lies. She knows now that it was him who had swung the golf club at her and it was him who had hit her under the overpass that night. And the woman who she had seen leaving in the car with him wasn't Anna. It was Megan.

Chapter 30 - Anna

Anna realizes who the voice on the phone belongs to and takes it outside, hurling it over the fence line. Tom is coming downstairs when she goes back in and she makes up a story about thinking she heard something outside. He compels her to go back to bed with him.

Chapter 31 - Rachel

Rachel goes to Tom and Anna's but no one answers the doorbell. She finds Anna and Evie out in the back garden. Tom is out with friends. She tells Anna they need to go.

Chapter 32 - Anna

Rachel interrogates Anna about how well she knows Tom's family and acquaintances, but it turns out that neither woman knows any of them. When she mentions Megan, Anna admits she knows that Tom had an affair with Megan, but tries to brush it off. They begin to uncover more of Tom's lies, and Anna has trouble thinking of herself and Rachel having such things in common. Rachel tells Anna about the baby Megan was carrying and the possibility that it could have been Tom's, encouraging Anna to take Evie and leave. Anna resists until Rachel mentions seeing Megan get into Tom's car on the night she disappeared. Rachel continues to try and convince Anna that Tom may have murdered Megan until both see him watching them from inside the house.

Chapter 33 - Megan

Megan realizes she is pregnant and suspects it's not Scott's baby, fearing he will find out the baby isn't his. She calls Kamal to beg him to come over. She confesses her pregnancy to him and her fears at being a mother again and about her future. Kamal assures her everything is going to be fine and gives her a friendly kiss as he departs. Megan decides to be honest about her situation. But when she does, she finds herself being choked. Escaping, she runs upstairs and locks herself into the bedroom. Scott begs for her forgiveness outside the door. She calls the baby's father from an old mobile phone and insists he meet her. When he does, he takes her away, but as Megan goes to him, she senses someone watching them from inside the underpass.

Chapter 34 - Rachel

Rachel confronts Tom about seeing him with Megan after he hit her in the underpass. Tom denies everything, attempting to paint Rachel as a liar, and Anna considers who to believe. She admits to finding Megan's phone, and Tom blames the affair on Anna having been consumed by their newborn daughter and uninterested in sex. Anna demands he hand Evie over to her, but he continues to rock the baby and keep her away from his wife until Anna is hysterical. Rachel instructs Anna to distract Tom while she calls the police, but just as she is dialing, he kicks her from behind and forces her back into the house.

Chapter 35 - Megan

Megan tells Tom that she is pregnant and that he is possibly the father. He tells her to get an abortion, claiming he does not want another child and that she would be a poor mother. She grows angry and starts yelling and pushing at him. Tom comes towards her and something hits her in the head. She realizes that her end is come.

Chapter 36 - Rachel

Tom refers to his affair with Megan as a little fun that ended when Megan started talking about running away together. She became obsessive, threatening to tell Anna about the affair. The night she disappeared, she asked to see Tom, and he blames Rachel for everything, as he was forced to go after her while she stumbled drunkenly through the neighborhood. He admits to hauling Rachel to the underpass and to hitting her to get her to stop crying. Then he happened upon Megan and they drove to the woods to talk. She told him about the pregnancy and he said he wasn't interested. When she started screaming at him, he hit her over the head with a rock. Realizing how injured she was, he decided he had to finish her off and then buried her. As Tom finishes his story, Rachel bolts, but he hits her over the head with a bottle and she falls unconscious.

Chapter 37 - Anna

Anna tries to convince herself that having Tom kill Rachel is what she wants so that the three of them can live in peace. But she knows she and Evie aren't safe with him since she knows he killed Megan. Rachel awakens, and Tom sends Anna back upstairs. She instead sits on the bottom stair with the phone in hand, waiting for the right opportunity.

Chapter 38 – Rachel

Rachel revives and Tom continues to blame her for the events that led to Megan's murder. He asks her what he should do with her and she feigns loving him still and promises to keep his secret. He taunts her by kissing her, and she plays along. She grabs something from a kitchen drawer and is able to distract him long enough to flee. He tackles her in the yard but she escapes again, running towards the train tracks. When he reaches her, she jams a corkscrew into his throat. Several weeks pass and Rachel reflects on how that day turned out. Anna had called an ambulance and the police, but Tom died before they arrived. When Gaskill and Riley questioned the women, Anna told them Rachel acted out of self-defense. As the media reports on Tom, it becomes more apparent that Tom lived a life of lies and Rachel didn't ever really know him at all. She thinks back on those last moments as Tom lay dying in the yard and remembers Anna running up. At first, Rachel thought she was trying to stop the bleeding, but then she realized that Anna was twisting the corkscrew deeper into his neck to ensure his death.

ANALYSIS OF KEY CHARACTER

Megan Hipwell is a haunted woman who cannot move beyond her transgressions to live a normal life. She is overwhelmed by her unhappiness, but mistakes it as boredom with her current situation instead of pain from deep psychic wounds.

Although she plays the role of the suburban housewife, her personal history is much darker than that. When her beloved brother passed away suddenly, she was overcome with grief and ran away – a pattern for her. She is not adept at working through her own emotions and instead will choose to run away from the situation, falsely believing that a fresh start and a new life will heal the pain. Having left home with limited resources forced her to make decisions that further dragged her down and beat up her self-worth. She experimented with prostitution and drug use, becoming pregnant.

Libby's death from Megan's negligence leaves her emotionally crippled. It also instills a fear in her that prevents her from wanting to start a family with Scott. She doesn't trust herself to be a mother again, to put another innocent child at risk. She has abandonment issues from the sudden loss of her brother and having her ex walk out on her after the death of their child. Perhaps this is why she always seems to have one foot out the door in regards to her marriage; if she leaves Scott first, then he cannot abandon her.

Megan is filled with self-loathing. She doesn't feel worthy of Scott's love andcannot take comfort in it. She is driven to look for other men, convinced the excitement of a love affair entices her. But the reality is she wants to feel needed and desired. She needs a constant reminder that she is accepted and loved. This is depicted best when she confesses her affair to Scott after discovering she is pregnant. She wants him to raise the baby with her. But when he grows angry over her admission, she switches gears and immediately turns to Tom for his support. Her desperate need to be accepted by a man ultimately leads to her death.

MAJOR SYMBOLS

A prominent piece of symbolism in *The Girl on the Train* is the train itself. For Rachel, the train symbolized a sense of security. She relies on its consistency and its direct course never to waver, a stability her own life does not possess at that period. Its constant motion is also representative of Rachel's inability to stay focused on rebuilding her life. As long as she keeps moving back and forth each day, she can pretend her life has a purpose, when in reality, she is just filling empty hours.

For Megan, the train signifies an escape, a line of tracks that carries its passengers to destinations unknown. She constantly romanticizes the idea of running away towards a new life, and the train is a visual reminder that such dreams are possible, if only she could gather up the nerve.

For Anna, the train is an obstruction of privacy. Passengers riding by watch her house as they pass. She lives in fear of Rachel's crazy intrusions into her life and never truly feels safe in her own home. Anna also holds contempt for the train because she knew Rachel had loved living alongside the tracks. That was just one more reminder that her home had originally belonged to Rachel, and she hated both the train and the home based on that principle alone.

MOTIFS

One of the reoccurring motifs in *The Girl on the Train* is adultery. It is woven throughout the book, altering the lives of each of the main characters in a multitude of ways. Rachel begins her story in a deep depression because of Tom's infidelity. His affair is the chief cause of their divorce, thus changing the course of Rachel's life forever.

Anna reflects on her affair with Tom with fond memories and admits she loved being a mistress and never felt any remorse for Rachel. But karma is vengeful, and Anna feels the hurt she once inflicted when she becomes aware of Tom's relationship with Megan.

Tom is the classic habitual adulterer. He makes excuses for himself by blaming his wives, first Rachel and then Anna, claiming their bad behavior drives him to stray. He never takes responsibility for his adulterous ways, much in the same way he blames Megan for losing his temper and doesn't take responsibility for her murder.

Megan's lack of self-worth is the motivator for her infidelity. She is overwhelmed by personal issues and uses physical connections with other men as an escape and a way to make herself feel valued. But it is never enough. Even as she is carrying on an affair with Tom, she is also attempting to seduce her therapist, Dr. Abdic.

THEMES

A theme of *The Girl on the Train* is deception. The relentless search for the truth drives the book and its characters; however, their personal deceptions prevent them from finding answers. They all wonder about the truth behind Megan's disappearance and then, ultimately, the truth behind her murder. But it is buried deep amidst their secrets, their lies, and their pretenses.

Rachel deceives herself by believing she can handle her alcohol and is going to get sober. Each day she convinces herself she is only going to have one drink, but she cannot stop, blacks out and has no recollection of events. By deceiving herself in this way, she cannot remember the timeline of events that occurred the night Megan disappeared while she was in Witney. Thus, possible clues and answers are lost to her.

Tom has deceived both Rachel and Anna with his infidelities. His affair with Megan is a deception he can never admit to once it is discovered that Megan is dead, as he knows he would become a suspect. Tom also used Rachel's drunken blackouts to twist the truth and convince her that he was a victim to her fits of rage while they were married. Because of this, she didn't realize until it was almost too late that he was the one who was violent and could be capable of murder.

Megan's deception involving her personal history came between her and Scott. Since Scott did not know many of the dark secrets from Megan's past, it was hard for him to understand her unhappiness and to consider she may have put herself in a dangerous situation. The deceit of Megan's affair with Tom has dire consequences, leading to her becoming pregnant with his baby and then to her murder.

CONCLUSION

The Girl on the Train is a simple title for a book containing an intricate plot that thrills with a suspenseful murder mystery sure to captivate all audiences. It's a remarkable breakout novel for Paula Hawkins, one that will leave readers begging for more.

THOUGHT PROVOKING /OR DISCUSSION QUESTIONS

To help guide further consideration of the text, the following questions might be useful. Answers to each can do much to help readers get more from the reading they do. Also a fantastic addition to anyone looking for ideas to share in their book club.

Author

- Does the author use his/her real name or a pseudonym? If the latter, what kind of person is implied by the pseudonym?
- What else has the author written? How does this book compare to the other things the author has written? Is it in the same genre?
- Is this book in a series the author writes? If so, where does it fit in the series?

Plot

- Is the plot a single, large piece?
- Is it made of several threads that move together? What unites the threads?
- Is it instead a series of short, less-connected pieces? What unites them?
- Does the plot start at the beginning of the action and move forward? Does it start in the middle and move back and forth from it? Does it follow another order entirely?
- What is the central conflict of the book? What drives it? What reasons do those on different sides of it have for their actions?
- Is the conflict person versus person, person versus nature, person versus society, person versus outside force or deity, person versus self or some other conflict?

Character

- Who is the narrator? Is it a first-person or third-person perspective? Is it limited or omniscient? What background and position does the narrator take? Is the narrator trustworthy?
- Who is the primary protagonist? What physical and psychological traits does the protagonist have?
- Who are major secondary protagonists? How do they relate to the primary protagonist? What physical and psychological traits do they have? How do they contribute to or take away from the primary protagonist?
- Who is the primary antagonist (If any)? What physical and psychological traits does the antagonist have? How does s/he oppose the protagonist?
- Who are major secondary antagonists? How do they relate to the primary antagonist? What physical and psychological traits do they have? How do they contribute to or take away from the primary antagonist? How do they oppose the protagonist?

Symbol and Motif

- When and where is the book set, or when and where is like the book is set? What associations attach to that time and place? What historical and literary events does the setting bring to mind? What associates with them?
- What colors are described most often? With what are they associated in the book? With what are they associated for you?
- Do the characters quote other books or works? What works? What lines do they quote? What associates with those quotations?
- What recurring patterns are in the text? Where do they appear: in narration, in character action, in character speech? How exactly do they repeat? How often do they repeat? With what do they associate?

Theme

- What messages does the book seem to send? How does it seem to send them?
- What social issues does the book seem to engage? How does it engage them? Are they relevant to you? Are they likely to be relevant to other readers?

Experience/Perspective/Response

• Did you feel drawn into the book immediately, or did it take time for you to get into the book? What in the book made you feel that way?

• Does anything in the book remind you of your own lived experience? What and how does it?

• How did the book make you feel overall? Satisfied? Confused? Angry? Happy? Content? Disturbed? • What in the book made you feel that way?

Ending

Did you find the ending satisfying?

- Would you change the ending? How?
- What would be the next chapter? Why?

29384513R00041

Made in the USA
San Bernardino, CA
20 January 2016